Outer Space

KU-753-560

Anne Rooney

Heinemann
LIBRARY

ABERDEENSHIRE LIBRARY AND
Rooney, Anne
Outer space /
Anne Rooney
J523.
1
2609097

www.heinemann.co.uk/library
Visit our website to find out more information about Heinemann Library books.

To order:

 Phone 44 (0) 1865 888066

 Send a fax to 44 (0) 1865 314091

 Visit the Heinemann Bookshop at www.heinemann.co.uk/library to browse our catalogue and order online.

Produced for Heinemann Library by

White-Thomson Publishing Ltd,
Bridgewater Business Centre,
210 High Street,
Lewes, East Sussex BN7 2NH

First published in Great Britain by Heinemann Library,
Jordan Hill, Oxford OX2 8EJ, part of Harcourt
Education Ltd.

© Harcourt Education Ltd 2008
The moral right of the proprietor has been asserted.

Anne Rooney asserts her moral right to be recognized
as the author of this work.

All rights reserved. No part of this publication may be
reproduced, stored in a retrieval system, or transmitted
in any form or by any means, electronic, mechanical,
photocopying, recording, or otherwise, without
either the prior written permission of the publishers or
a licence permitting restricted copying in the United
Kingdom issued by the Copyright Licensing Agency Ltd,
90 Tottenham Court Road, London W1T 4LP
(www.cla.co.uk).

Consultant: Paul Roche
Commissioning Editors: Sarah Shannon and
    Steve White-Thomson
Editor: Sonya Newland
Design: Tim Mayer
Artwork: William Donohoe

Originated by Chroma Graphics (Overseas) Pte. Ltd.
Printed in China by South China Printing Co. Ltd.

ISBN 978 0 431 90745 1
12 11 10 09 08
10 9 8 7 6 5 4 3 2 1

British Library Cataloguing in Publication Data
Rooney, Anne
    Outer space. - (Earth's final frontiers)
    1. Outer space - Juvenile literature 2. Outer space -
    Exploration - Juvenile literature
    I. Title
    520

Acknowledgements
The author and publisher would like to thank the
following for allowing their pictures to be reproduced
in this publication:
Corbis: 9 (Hans Schmied/zefa), 23t (Bettmann),
32b (Roger Ressmeyer); **iStock:** 6 (Bryan Busovicki);
NASA: 10, 11, 12t, 12b, 13 (JPL/Cornell), 14, 15, 16,
19 (Space Telescope Science Institute), 20, 22, 26t,
26b, 28, 29, 30, 31 (Bill Ingalls), 32t (JPL-Caltech/Max
Planck Institute), 34, 36, 37, 38, 40, 41; **Science Photo
Library:** 17 (JPL-Caltech/UMD), 18 (NASA/ESA/STSCI/
R.ALBRECHT, ST-ECF), 23b (Pascal Goetgheluck), 24
(RIA Novosti), 32 (Dr Juerg Alean), 35 (NASA), 39
(Geoff Tompkinson); **TopFoto:** 7 (Fortean), 8 (Topham
Picturepoint), 25.

Cover image courtesy of David Ducros/Science Photo
Library.

Every effort has been made to contact copyright holders
of any material reproduced in this book. Any omissions
will be rectified in subsequent printings if notice is given
to the publishers.

Disclaimer
All the Internet addresses (URLs) given in this book were
valid at the time of going to press. However, due to the
dynamic nature of the Internet, some addresses may
have changed, or sites may have ceased to exist since
publication. While the author and publishers regret
any inconvenience this may cause readers, no
responsibility for any such changes can be accepted
by either the author or the publishers.

Aberdeenshire Library and Information Service
www.aberdeenshire.gov.uk/libraries
Renewals Hotline 01224 661511

1 1 SEP 2009

1 6 AUG 2012

2 1 DEC 2016

Rooney, Anne

Outer space /
Anne Rooney

J523.
1

2609097

ALIS

2609097

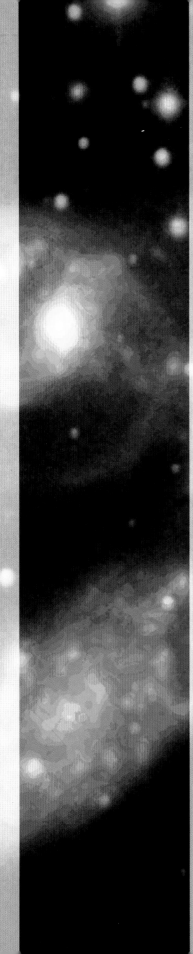

CONTENTS

Words appearing in the text in bold, **like this**, are explained in the glossary.

THE SOLAR SYSTEM

Our **solar system** is made up of eight **planets**, including
Earth, all revolving around an ordinary star – the sun. Beyond
our own **galaxy**, the Milky Way, lie countless other stars, solar
systems, and galaxies. Although Earth's **moon** is the only
space body that humans have set foot on at the moment,
exploration of space has gone much further, thanks
to technology that has allowed scientists to see
what is happening far away in space.

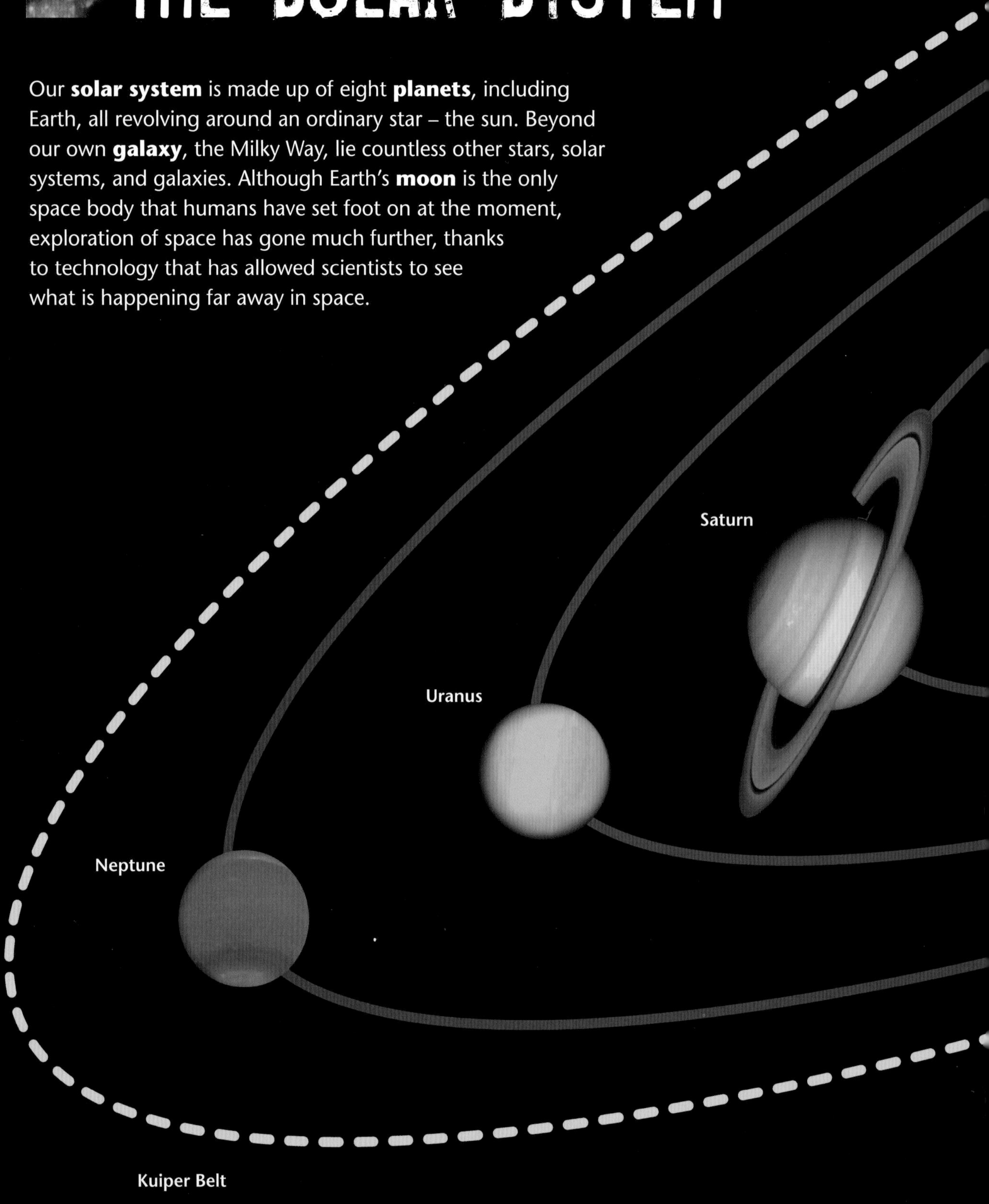

Saturn

Uranus

Neptune

Kuiper Belt

Sun

Mercury

Venus

Earth

Mars

Moon

Jupiter

Asteroid Belt

The distances between bodies in outer space are vast. Our closest neighbouring star, Proxima Centauri, is 40 trillion, or 40,000,000,000,000 kilometres (km) (25,000,000,000,000 miles) from Earth. Numbers like this are difficult to use, so astronomers use **light years** or **Astronomical Units** (AU) to measure distances in space. One Astronomical Unit is the distance from Earth to the sun.

FRONTIERS BEYOND THE SKY

The television series *Star Trek* promised viewers adventures beyond the "final frontier", "where no man has gone before". A frontier is an exciting, challenging, and often dangerous boundary. It is the area where familiar territory gives way to the unknown. On Earth, early **pioneers** crossed frontiers into unexplored lands and seas. They discovered strange animals and plants, wild and exotic landscapes, and people with unfamiliar customs and languages.

As more land became known, the frontiers were pushed further back, to the most remote places on Earth. These included the deep sea, jungles, deserts, mountain ranges, the polar ice caps, and the inside of the Earth.

▼ *Even early people had some knowledge of astronomy. Stonehenge in Wiltshire, England, was made more than 4,000 years ago. The arrangement of the stones suggests the builders had a basic understanding of how the planets moved.*

EARLY INVESTIGATIONS

Even before the invention of the telescope, early scientists tracked the movements of the planets across the sky. Stone circles like Stonehenge in the United Kingdom demonstrate that early people realized bodies in space moved in a particular way. In Baghdad (now in Iraq) and later in Cairo (Egypt), early Arab astronomers made precise measurements. They used massive instruments, including quarter circles 7.6 metres (m) (25 feet [ft]) across, and a metal model of the **orbits** of the planets. Their measurements, made as early as the eighth century, were remarkably accurate and were used by other astronomers for hundreds of years.

FASCINATING SKIES

Space remains the greatest frontier for humans. A vast universe, in which humans are taking their first exploratory steps, stretches in all directions around our planet. No human has yet been further than the moon. Even our own solar system is still largely unknown.

People have always wondered about the stars and planets they can see in the night sky. Throughout history, people have used myths, legends, religion, and science to try to explain them. We now know that space extends unimaginable distances around us, but even this is a recent discovery.

REACHING OUT

Four hundred years ago, the first telescopes gave people the chance to begin exploring space. They saw that the planets were other worlds, and space became a frontier that might one day be explored. Since then, telescopes of different types have been built, which can look deep into outer space, beyond our own solar system. People have travelled into space and to the surface of the moon. Unmanned spacecraft have gone even further than this.

With the spacecraft that are currently available, humans will not be able to travel beyond the solar system in the near future because the distances involved are so great. Using technology, however, we can begin to explore a little of what lies beyond that frontier. With special telescopes it is possible to gather and **analyse** information from deep space. It is also possible to send information out into space in the hope that, like early pioneers on Earth, we may one day encounter beings who will understand us.

▼ *Armillary spheres were invented by the Greek astronomer Eratosthenes in the third century BC and have been used for more than 2,000 years. They show how the stars and planets seem to move in relation to the Earth.*

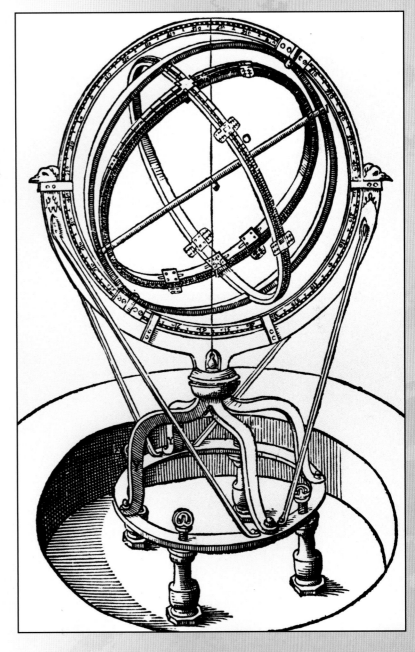

VOYAGES OF DISCOVERY

For more than 40 years people have travelled in space and used technology to explore the other planets and moons of the solar system. We still know less about them than we do about even the most remote areas on Earth. Yet the emerging picture suggests a huge variety of other worlds, almost unimaginably different from our own.

OUR SOLAR SYSTEM

The solar system is the area of space affected by the **gravity** of the sun and the **solar wind**. Within it lie the sun, the planets, and their moons.

A planet is a body that orbits the sun. It is large enough to have its own gravity and to have drawn in any smaller chunks of rock in its area. There are eight planets. Four are the **terrestrial** planets – Mercury, Venus, Earth, and Mars. These have a hard, rocky surface and are closest to the sun. The other four – Jupiter, Saturn, Uranus, and Neptune – are called **gas giants**. They are huge balls of gas that have no solid surface. Together, the four gas giants account for 99 percent of the **mass** of all the planets.

Until August 2006, Pluto was considered a planet, but it is now called a dwarf planet or **planetoid**. Pluto lies further from the sun than the eight planets. It is a cold, dark, solid world, and astronomers know very little about it.

All the planets except Venus and Mercury have moons. These are natural **satellites** that orbit the planets. All moons are solid and some are as small as 1–2 km (0.6–1.2 miles) in diameter. Some planets have lots of moons. Jupiter has 63 moons that are large enough to have been given a name or number, many of them less than 10 km (6 miles) across. Saturn has the most large moons, with 31 over 10 km (6 miles) in diameter, and 56 in total known so far. Both of these planets probably have many more small moons that have not yet been discovered.

▲ The Bayeux Tapestry, made after the Norman victory at the Battle of Hastings in 1066, shows a comet that is thought to be Halley's Comet.

DISCOVERY OF THE PLANETS

Ancient times:	Venus, Mars, Jupiter, Saturn, and Mercury
1781:	Uranus
1846:	Neptune
1930:	Pluto

MORE ROCKS AND ICE

As well as planets and moons, billions of much smaller lumps of rock and ice orbit the sun. These are **asteroids**, **meteoroids**, and **comets**. Asteroids are large chunks of rock or iron (or both). The largest, Ceres, is 933 km (580 miles) across. Most lie in the **Asteroid Belt** between Mars and Jupiter. Meteoroids are smaller lumps of rock. If they fall to Earth, they are called **meteorites**. Comets are clumps of rock, dust, and ice with streaming tails of dust millions of kilometres long when they pass close to the sun.

DISCOVERING SPACE BODIES

All the planets were first seen from Earth. Some moons were first seen from Earth, too, but others have been discovered through telescopes in space or by spacecraft flying past the planets. For thousands of years, people have seen comets streak across the sky and **meteors** burning as they fall through the atmosphere without really understanding what they were. Only the largest asteroids are visible from Earth. Our knowledge of these bodies has come with space travel and modern telescopes.

▲ *This iron meteorite, known as the Hoba meteorite, was found in Namibia, Africa, in 1920. It is thought to have reached Earth 80,000 years ago. At 60,000 kilograms (kg) (132,276 pounds [lbs]), it is the heaviest known meteorite.*

9

PROBING SPACE

Information about the solar system has been discovered by sending out spacecraft to explore it. Knowledge about space beyond our solar system has come from using telescopes and other instruments.

All spacecraft that have travelled further than the moon have been **probes** – unmanned craft that carry equipment and robotic tools. Some carry out **flyby** missions, flying close to a planet or moon to take photographs and measurements. Others carry **landers**, which are dropped on to the surface to take readings, examine samples, and take photographs. Probes do not return to Earth, but send the data and images they collect back to Earth by radio.

Optical telescopes use light to show an image. Radio telescopes collect **radio waves** that come from distant stars and galaxies. They use these to "see" what is in outer space. Huge telescopes are placed on high land and even on satellites in space to avoid **light pollution** or distortion from Earth's atmosphere.

▼ *An artist's impression of the* Cassini *spacecraft releasing the* Huygens *probe over Titan, one of Saturn's moons, at the start of its mission to discover more about this ringed planet.*

INVESTIGATING THE PLANETS

Several probes were sent to single planets as early as the 1960s. The first was the Soviet *Venera 1*, which flew past Venus in 1961, in the very early years of space travel. The communication link failed, though, and no information was gained. More recently, probes have carried out much longer missions and some have visited more than one planet. Several have landed on Mars, *Cassini-Huygens* has visited Saturn (2005), and *Galileo* has studied Jupiter (1996).

The *Cassini-Huygens* mission is the first to explore Saturn's moons and rings from within orbit around the planet. *Cassini* (the orbiter) arrived at Saturn in 2004 and the lander, *Huygens*, landed on the moon Titan in 2005. They will spend four years investigating Saturn.

The *Galileo* probe was launched in 1989 and sent the first close-up images of an asteroid, Gaspra, in 1991. It also sent back images of a collision between a comet and a planet, when the comet Shoemaker-Levy 9 crashed into Jupiter. *Galileo*'s most exciting discovery, however, related to Jupiter's moon, Europa. The probe confirmed the presence of liquid water beneath Europa's surface. This means it may host some form of life.

WHO'S WHO

Galileo Galilei

Galileo Galilei (1564–1642) was an Italian scientist and astronomer. He heard about telescopes that had been recently invented by the Dutch, and decided to build his own. He was the first person to look at the planets with a telescope, the first to discover moons around another planet, and the first person to recognize the Milky Way as a huge collection of stars. The Roman Catholic Church did not allow Galileo to teach that the Earth orbits the sun, but on his deathbed he announced that he still believed it to be true. The Church only withdrew its objection in 1992.

DESTINATION: DEEP SPACE

Perhaps the most exciting and intriguing missions are those that head into the unknown, beyond the frontiers of our own solar system. Two early missions sent by the U.S. Space Agency NASA are heading out into deep space. *Pioneers 10* and *11* were launched in 1972 and 1973. They have flown past the gas giants and are now no longer in communication with Earth. The last contact was with *Pioneer 10* in 2003. It is heading towards the star Aldebaran, but – if it survives – it will take two million years to arrive.

The twin probes *Voyagers 1* and *2* were launched in 1977. They followed a similar path to the *Pioneers* at first, and have now overtaken them. *Voyager 1* is now 100 AU from the sun – 100 times the distance of Earth from the sun. It will still take 40,000 years to cross into **interstellar** space. It is still in communication with Earth and it may stay in contact for another 20 years, but it will probably keep travelling long after that. Since overtaking *Pioneer*'s distance from the sun, *Voyager* has sent information about the magnetic field and particles beyond the planets. It has taken longer to reach the edges of the solar system than expected, telling scientists that the sun's influence extends further than they thought.

▲ *The Hubble Space Telescope is an optical telescope that orbits Earth as a satellite. Launched in 1990, it has provided striking pictures of objects in deep space that have added immensely to human knowledge of the universe.*

THE TERRESTRIAL PLANETS

▼ *This image of Venus was produced by the NASA Magellan probe, which used radar to map the surface through the thick clouds of the atmosphere. The colour has been added by computer, using information from the Russian Venera 13 and 14 landers.*

MERCURY

Mercury is the planet closest to the sun. It is scorching hot by day, 427°C (801°F), but freezing at night, –173°C (–279°F), as it has no atmosphere to hold in the warmth from the sun. One day on Mercury is 58.6 Earth days.

The U.S. probe *Mariner 10* flew past Mercury three times in 1974–75, and photographed 45 percent of its surface. As Mercury turns slowly on its **axis**, the same side was visible all the time. The other side, turned away from the sun, was in darkness and could not be photographed. The pictures show a rocky landscape like that of Earth's moon, with craters up to 1,300 km (800 miles) wide. There are vast, flat plains, evidence of lava flows, and towering **scarps**, cliffs, and mountain ranges caused by the surface cooling, shrinking, and cracking.

VENUS

Venus lies between Mercury and Earth, but it is very different from them. Searing heat, 464°C (867°F), and a thick, acidic atmosphere at immense pressure make it an impossible place for a spacecraft to survive for long. It has been described as "the closest thing to hell in the solar system".

Venus was first explored by the Soviet *Venera* missions. Probes have dropped balloons to investigate the atmosphere and sent landers that can survive for a short time to examine the surface. The atmosphere is too thick to see through, but the U.S. *Pioneer 1* (1978–92) and *Magellan* (1990–94) missions have used **radar** to map the surface, revealing towering mountains and evidence of volcanic eruptions.

▶ *Mercury is the planet closest to the sun. So far, we have only been able to take images of one side of Mercury, because of the way it turns on its axis. The Messenger probe will go into orbit around Mercury in 2011 and take images of the "dark" side.*

MARS

Mars is rocky and cold, at –87 to –5°C (–125 to 23°F). Although Venus is closer to Earth than Mars, Mars is likely to be the first planet visited by humans. Its rocky surface, and the atmospheric pressure and temperature, make it more suitable for exploration. Landers and **astronauts** will be able to move around on the surface using technologies already developed for the moon landings. The temperature, pressure, and acidic atmosphere on Venus would make it impossible for astronauts to explore.

There have been 35 missions to Mars, but not all have been successful. By the end of 2006 there were six spacecraft studying Mars, either on the ground or in orbit – the most ever to have been active around another planet.

There is at least a small amount of water on Mars. It is present as a gas in the atmosphere and freezes as frost on the surface. There is also evidence that there was a lot more water on Mars in the past and there may be ice underground. For many years people have wondered if there could be life on Mars. There are no large life forms, but we might still find **microbes** on Mars.

EXPLORING MARS

1965: *Mariner 4* (U.S.) takes the first images of Mars.

1971: Mars Orbiter/Lander 3 (Soviet Union) makes the first landing. It sends a video from the surface for 20 seconds.

1976: *Vikings 1* and *2* (U.S.) send 52,000 images, carry out soil experiments, and record data about the atmosphere. They find that the soil is similar to some rocks found on Earth, but do not discover any signs of life in the soil.

1997: Mars Global Surveyor (U.S.) maps the entire surface and discovers predictable annual weather patterns.

1997: Mars Pathfinder (U.S.) examines soil and rock, studies wind and weather, and sends images of the surface. Its findings reveal that Mars once had a warmer, wetter climate, and a thicker atmosphere – conditions better suited to life than current conditions on Mars.

2003: Mars Exploration Rovers *Spirit* and *Opportunity* (U.S.) send more than 170,000 high-resolution images. Using photographs taken by orbiters, the mission selects regions for the landers to investigate. They explore craters and ancient sand dunes, and examine layered rock that gives an insight into the history of rocks and weather conditions on Mars.

2006: Mars Reconnaissance Orbiter (U.S.) takes images of the surface and looks for future landing sites for surface rovers.

▼ *The surface of Mars photographed from a Mars Exploration Rover (MER), showing a feature called Victoria Crater. The rocks and dust of the surface are given their reddish colour by the rust (iron oxide) they contain.*

THE GAS GIANTS

JUPITER

Jupiter is over 1,000 times the volume of Earth and makes up two thirds of the mass of all the planets in the solar system on its own. Most of our information about Jupiter has come from the *Galileo* probe (1996), though it was first photographed by the *Pioneer* and *Voyager* missions.

The atmosphere of a gas giant can be turbulent, with great winds and lightning storms. Jupiter's Great Red Spot is a massive storm that has been raging for at least 300 years, although no one knows why it is red. The *Galileo* probe investigated the atmosphere and took **infrared** images of the spot that revealed individual clouds up to 50 km (31 miles) thick. More information will be discovered when the *New Horizons* mission flies past Jupiter in 2007.

▼ *The Great Red Spot (seen here at top left) is a huge storm in Jupiter's atmosphere. At its widest, it is three times as wide as the Earth. Winds at the edge of the storm can reach 400 kmh (250 mph).*

◀ This image of Saturn's rings was taken by Cassini, which has been studying the rings since 2005. The different colours are the result of different **wavelengths** of light, and some look brighter than others.

SATURN

Saturn is the second-largest planet in the solar system. It is less dense than water – if dropped into a large enough bath, it would float. Like Jupiter, Saturn is stormy, with winds that blow at up to 1,770 kilometres per hour (kmh) (1,100 miles per hour [mph]).

All the gas giants have rings – orbiting clouds of tiny dust particles, rocks, or chunks of ice. Saturn has the most spectacular system of rings. They were first investigated by *Pioneer 11* in 1979 and more recently by *Cassini-Huygens* in 2006. They seem to be made of small chunks of ice ranging from a few centimetres to several metres across. They may contain a mix of icy comets caught by Saturn's gravity, and the remains of shattered moons and asteroids.

MYSTERIOUS WORLDS

Neptune and Uranus have been visited only by *Voyager 2*, and no spacecraft has ever visited Pluto. These bodies remain mysterious and fascinating because very little is known about them. The NASA mission *New Horizons* is set to uncover some of the secrets of Pluto and its moon, Charon. Launched in 2006, it will reach Pluto in 2015.

Uranus has 27 named moons, 10 discovered by *Voyager 2*. The planet is tilted on its side, and may have been knocked over by a collision in the past. Its rings seem to be made up of ice boulders.

Neptune has rings of dust, and several spots. Like the Great Red Spot on Jupiter, these are vast storms that have been raging for years. The largest is as big as Earth and has the fiercest winds anywhere in the solar system, blowing at up to 2,000 kmh (1,200 mph).

HOW GASSY IS A GAS GIANT?

A substance can exist as a solid, a liquid, or a gas depending on temperature and pressure. In a solid, particles are close together and move very little. In a liquid, they are further apart and can move more freely. In a gas, the particles are widely spaced and very mobile. As temperature rises, solids melt into liquids and liquids become gases. At high pressures, though, particles are squashed together. At very high pressures, just as at very low temperatures, gases become liquids or even solids. At the huge pressures inside gas giants, gases may exist as a slushy, near-solid liquid.

FINAL FRONTIERS

Although we know quite a lot about our own moon and our neighbour Mars, much of the rest of the solar system remains a mystery. The more remote and hostile environments in it represent frontiers that we are only just beginning to explore.

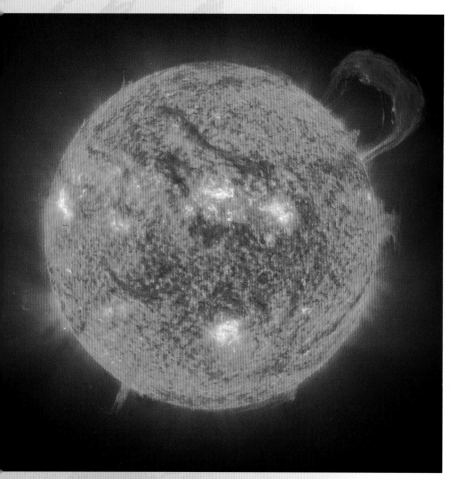

▲ *The sun photographed by SOHO, showing a flare of electrically charged gas (plasma) erupting from the surface.*

THE SUN

The sun is a massive ball of hot gases 1.3 million times the size of the Earth. The temperature on the surface is 5,800°C (10,470°F), so no spacecraft could ever land there. Scientists study the chemistry of the sun, and use telescopes in space and on Earth to look at it. It is dangerous to look directly at the sun, so special tools are needed to study it.

SOHO – the SOlar and **Heliospheric** Observatory – is a satellite in orbit around the sun, a million miles from Earth. SOHO gathers images of the sun and studies patterns of **radiation** and **sound waves** to find out what is happening inside it and on its surface.

SOLAR WIND

The sun has violent storms, and sometimes throws out plumes of gas and radiation that reach as far as Earth and way beyond. Particles shot out of the sun form what is called the solar wind. This can disrupt spacecraft and communications systems on Earth, so studying and predicting the solar wind is important. SOHO is able to spot **turbulence** even when it is on the side of the sun facing away from Earth.

Studying the solar wind can also reveal what the sun is made of. NASA's spacecraft *Genesis* (2001–04) collected particles of the solar wind weighing no more than a few grains of salt, which it returned to Earth. They are still being examined.

EMPTY SPACE?

The space between and beyond the planets in our solar system is not empty. There are asteroids, meteoroids, comets, and dust, as well as particles of the solar wind. Most asteroids can be found in the Asteroid Belt, which lies between Mars and Jupiter, though a few cross Earth's orbit. These asteroids are the remnants of material left over from when the solar system formed. Just as we can sometimes judge what a building is like on the inside from the debris left at a building site, so we can find out about the solar system by examining the left-over matter.

▼ *A projectile weighing 372 kg (820 lbs) and launched by the* Deep Impact *spacecraft crashes into comet Tempel-1, producing a shower of ice and rock, and leaving a crater in the surface of the comet.*

ASTEROID ATTACK!

Small meteorites fall to Earth all the time – but a large one (an asteroid) could do huge damage. Many scientists believe that the dinosaurs died out after an asteroid at least 15 km (10 miles) across hit Earth. The atmosphere filled with dust, blocking out the sun and so killing most plant and animal life. Although several asteroids look as though they may come close to Earth, none is on a direct collision course yet.

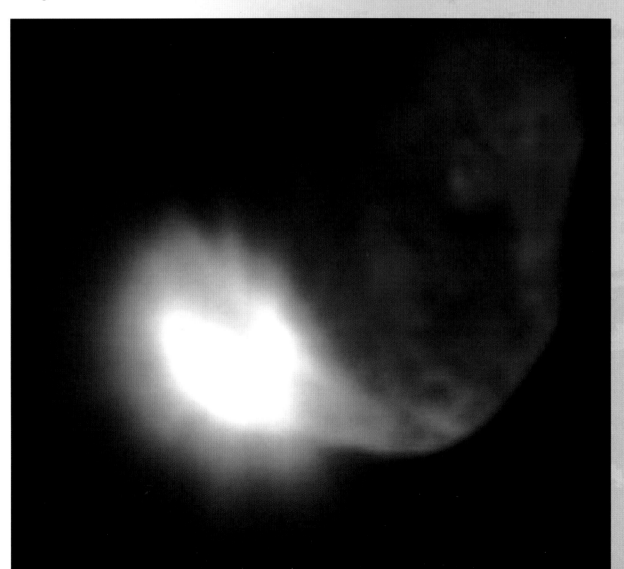

STUDYING ASTEROIDS

There are around 340,000 known asteroids in the Asteroid Belt, but there may be many more – perhaps millions. Asteroids range from a few metres to hundreds of kilometres across. Scientists estimate there may be 750,000 that are more than 1 km (0.6 mile) across. So far, 134,181 have been named or numbered. Some even have their own tiny moons. The *Galileo* probe passed through the Asteroid Belt in 1991. It took the first close-up images of asteroids, including one of the asteroid Ida and its moon, Dactyl. This was the first discovery of an asteroid with a moon.

COMET CHASERS

Comets formed at the start of the solar system, 4,500 million years ago, and are unchanged since then. There may be a trillion comets spread through the solar system. They are particles of dust and rock frozen in ice, with a tail of dust and gas. Most orbit the sun in the **Oort Cloud** – a huge region of icy bodies thought to extend halfway to the next star, Proxima Centauri – and in the **Kuiper Belt**. We only know about a few of them because they only reflect light when they are close enough to the sun, so we can't see them when they are far away. They orbit like planets. In 2006, the U.S. probe *Stardust* collected a sample of a comet's dust. The **European Space Agency**'s probe *Rosetta*, launched in 2004, is scheduled to make the first landing on a comet in 2014, on Comet 67P/Churyumov-Gerasimenko.

PLUTO

All we know about Pluto comes from observations with telescopes and from measurements made when Earth was lined up with the orbit of one of Pluto's moons, Charon, in 1985–90. Scientists measured light reflected from the surface and produced a map. The *New Horizons* probe should provide the first close-up pictures of the planet. There is not enough light there to take ordinary images, so it will use infrared and **ultraviolet imagers**.

THE SEARCH FOR STARDUST

Stardust was launched in 1999 to fly close to comet Wild-2 and gather dust samples from it. During its journey, *Stardust* travelled a total of 4.6 billion km (2.8 billion miles). The sample it brought back contains not only dust from the comet, but also a few grains of interstellar dust. Early results show that the composition of the dust is not what scientists expected. The comet seems to contain matter from the inner solar system. Astronomers may have to reassess theories about the history of the solar system.

▼ *The European Space Agency's Faint Object Camera took these pictures of the planetoid Pluto and its moon Charon.*

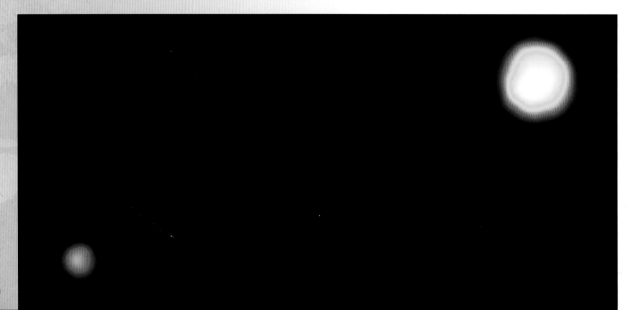

SEDNA

The planetoid Sedna, discovered in 2004, is on average around three times as far from the sun as Pluto. It may be part of the Oort Cloud. In 72 years time, Sedna's orbit will bring it as close to Earth as it ever gets. This will give scientists their best chance to investigate it for 10,500 years – the time it takes Sedna to orbit the sun.

BEYOND THE EDGES

The very edge of the solar system, where the sun's gravity finally becomes too weak to have any effect, forms the boundary with interstellar space. Our solar system is only one star system out of hundreds of billions in our galaxy, the Milky Way. And there are many more galaxies. Travelling to them is beyond our capabilities at the moment.

As technology improves it opens up possibilities for finding ever-more distant objects, pushing the frontiers of the universe still further away. The most distant known object at the moment is a galaxy called Abell 1835 IR1916, which lies more than 13 billion light years away. This is a galaxy forming in the early years of the universe. As it has taken more than 13 billion years for the light from the galaxy to reach Earth, we are able to see it as it was long ago – we won't be able to see it in its current state for another 13 billion years or so.

▲ *A distant galaxy – NGC 3079 – photographed by the Hubble Space Telescope. It is 50 million light years from Earth, in the* **constellation** *Ursa Major.*

NOT AN EASY RIDE

Space is the most difficult, dangerous, and expensive frontier to explore. To send people into space is the most ambitious and exciting undertaking humans have ever attempted. Despite the dangers, hundreds of thousands of people dream of becoming astronauts – yet only 450 people had been into space by the end of 2006.

▼ *The rocket* Friendship 7 *is launched from the Kennedy Space Center in 1962. This was the first American manned orbital space flight.*

ROCKET SCIENCE

A spacecraft needs a huge burst of energy to escape from Earth's gravity. Spacecraft are launched using rockets powered by an explosive chemical reaction. Lots of fuel is burned very quickly, sending out a jet of exhaust gases that forces the rocket upwards.

After lift-off, the rocket falls away, dropping back to Earth to fall into the ocean. The spacecraft has a covering, called a faring, which gives it a streamlined shape to help it move through the atmosphere. This, too, is dropped once the craft has passed into space. Further rockets boost the spacecraft into the correct orbit, or on the next stage of its journey. Since there is no oxygen in space, the craft must carry tanks of liquid oxygen to burn its fuel. As the tanks and rockets are used up, they are dropped. Space Shuttles (see page 29) are launched on the back of a rocket that works in a similar way.

Rockets were first developed as weapons, and were only later used to blast satellites into orbit. A satellite must be launched with enough power to reach a height of at least 200 km (128 miles), and to travel at the right speed to stay in orbit. It will then orbit Earth rather than falling back down or escaping into space.

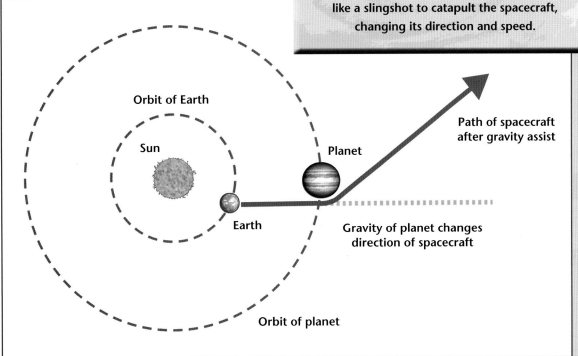

BOUNCING OFF PLANETS

Spacecraft get a boost from planets whenever they can. The route is planned to use the **gravitational fields** of planets and the sun in a gravity-assist move. This uses gravity rather like a slingshot to catapult the spacecraft, changing its direction and speed.

Orbit of Earth

Sun

Planet

Path of spacecraft after gravity assist

Earth

Gravity of planet changes direction of spacecraft

Orbit of planet

▲ *This diagram shows how a spacecraft uses the gravity of the sun and a planet to alter its path through space.*

FAR, FAR AWAY

Distances in space are immense, and journeys take a very long time. *Voyager 2* travelled for 12 years at an average speed of 68,400 kmh (42,750 mph) to reach Neptune. For unmanned craft, the problems with such long journeys are largely practical. If the craft needs to fire rocket boosters, it must carry the fuel and oxygen with it. It may carry a lander, which it must launch at the right time, and it must navigate its own course correctly. Mistakes mean the failure of the mission, wasting millions of dollars and years of research effort, although scientists certainly learn from these mistakes.

Manned spacecraft face additional problems. Mistakes or accidents far from Earth could lead to the death of the crew. People need food, water, and air – all of which must be carried or made on board. They need to get rid of their waste, deal with any health problems, and cope with the psychological difficulties of being cooped up in a tiny spacecraft. Problems that seem mundane on Earth – missing home, being bored, falling out with colleagues, or distress at long periods of isolation – could threaten the success of a long-term space mission.

KEEP ON GOING!

Spacecraft travelling near the sun can use solar panels to convert the sun's energy to electricity and to move them along. Further away, however, there is not enough sunlight for this to work. Craft such as *Voyager* are nuclear powered – they produce electricity from the decay of **radioactive** material.

Ion propulsion is a new way of powering a spacecraft. A high-speed stream of **ions** (charged particles) pushes the craft along. It uses very gentle thrust, no more than the pressure of a sheet of paper on your hand, but it is constant, so that although the craft accelerates slowly, it eventually reaches high speeds. Future spacecraft may use sails so that they can be pushed along by the solar wind or even by **photons** (particles of light energy).

STAYING IN TOUCH

Spacecraft communicate with Earth by radio, but even radio waves take a long time to travel great distances. Radio signals from *Voyager 1*, nearing the edge of the solar system, now take 13 hours to reach Earth – *Voyager 1* is therefore 13 light hours from Earth. This means that a craft or its crew on a manned mission would need to be able to handle any emergency situations without help from Earth. Sophisticated computer programming aims to help spacecraft make decisions in unexpected circumstances.

HOSTILE WORLDS

Hostile environments are a major problem facing landers on other worlds. Very high or very low temperatures, corrosive atmospheres – such as the atmosphere on Venus, which is rich in sulphuric acid – and fierce storms present great challenges. Landers on Venus have been crushed by the huge pressure of the atmosphere after only a few minutes.

Manned spacecraft could most easily land on planets that have an atmospheric pressure that is similar to or lower than that on Earth. They would also need bearable temperatures and relatively gentle weather in order for humans to survive there. Crew landing on such a planet would still need spacesuits, however, and an air supply, as nowhere that we know of in the solar system has a breathable atmosphere.

SPACESUITS

Gold-coated visor reduces glare

Survival pack contains liquid oxygen and water to cool inner garment

Gloves have silicone fingertips to give some sense of touch

Control module on chest to regulate oxygen and water

Outer pressure garment has six layers

Inner garment is cooled by circulating water

SICK IN SPACE

Space can make astronauts sick. In space, far away from the strong gravity of a planet, bones do not have to support the weight of the body and they grow weaker. Muscles, including the heart, begin to waste away, becoming smaller and weaker. Blood cells also reduce – astronauts lose up to a fifth of their red blood cells.

Microbes grow more quickly in space where there is no gravity, and astronauts are more likely to fall ill in space as their **immune systems** work less well.

Anyone on a space flight may fall sick with normal illnesses, too. Robotic surgical tools that can be controlled at a distance may be used on long-distance missions, so that surgeons on Earth can carry out operations in an emergency.

A more alarming possibility is that alien microbes may cause illnesses that have never been seen before. Some scientists believe that microbes may be carried through space on meteorites, and they may exist on other planets.

▲ *The* Apollo 11 *astronauts – Buzz Aldrin, Neil Armstrong, and Michael Collins – in a quarantine trailer after the first successful moon landing in 1969.*

▼ *Robots like the Da Vinci surgical robot can perform detailed operations. It has "wrists" that have the same level of movement as a human wrist, and it can be manipulated by a surgeon.*

FACE TO FACE WITH SPACE

For centuries, people have dreamed of visiting the stars. Now, that dream is being realized as humans begin to explore this final frontier. It took little more than 10 years from humans first venturing into space to taking the first steps on the moon.

◄ Early space travellers were crammed into extremely small capsules. The aim of these first flights was just to prove that it was possible to get a human into space and safely back again.

BLAST OFF!

The very first spacecraft was a tiny satellite called *Sputnik 1*, launched by the Soviet Union in October 1957. It was a sphere 58 centimetres (cm) (23 inches [in]) across and weighed only 83.6 kg (184 lbs). *Sputnik* orbited Earth for two months before burning up as it re-entered Earth's atmosphere.

The United States was shocked that the Soviet Union had reached space first, and rushed to launch a satellite of its own. *Vanguard TV3*, launched in December 1957, rose just over 1 m (4 ft) before crashing to the ground and exploding. The first successful launch was *Explorer 1* in 1958.

For the next 30 years, the United States and the Soviet Union competed to conquer space before finally beginning to work together. The **space race** became a focus of the Cold War – the hostility between the two nations that lasted from the end of World War II until 1991. Both countries were determined to get to the moon first.

WHO'S WHO

Yuri Gagarin
Yuri Gagarin (1934–68) trained as a pilot with the Soviet Air Force. In 1961 he made his only space flight, but he became a national hero and internationally famous. He was killed during a routine training flight in an aircraft in 1968.

THE FIRST COSMONAUTS

The Russian Yuri Gagarin became the first man in space in April 1961. He spent one hour and 48 minutes in *Vostok 1*, orbiting Earth. The first American in space was Alan Shepard in May 1961. He made a 15-minute flight below the height for orbit. The first U.S. astronaut to orbit Earth was John Glenn in February 1962. The first woman in space was the Russian **cosmonaut** Valentina Tereshkova in 1963.

In their own words ...

"I could have gone on flying through space forever."
Yuri Gagarin

SPACE ANIMALS

Animals were sent into space to test whether it would be safe to send people. A month after *Sputnik 1*, *Sputnik 2* carried the first passenger into space – a dog called Laika. Laika died, as there was no plan for bringing the satellite back to Earth. In 1960, *Sputnik 5* carried two dogs, 40 mice, two rats, and some plants into space, all of which came back alive. In 1961, the chimpanzee Ham was sent into space in a U.S. *Mercury* capsule.

▲ Sputnik 2, *with the dog Laika, before the craft was launched in November 1957. Although Laika died, later experiments with animals proved it was possible to bring living creatures safely back to Earth.*

AIMING FOR THE MOON

As soon as it was clear that people could go into space and survive, the race was on to reach the moon. The U.S. programme began with the simple *Mercury* capsules used by Shepard and Glenn, and then moved on to the more advanced *Gemini* craft. Astronauts practised all the moves needed to get a spacecraft to the moon. They learned how to change orbits, steer a craft in space, dock craft (bring two craft together in space), and carry out **spacewalks**. The Soviet cosmonauts did the same using their *Soyuz* craft. The Soviet Union was also secretly developing a giant rocket and a spacecraft to land on the moon.

▲ *Astronaut Buzz Aldrin leaves the lander to step on to the surface of the moon, 20 July 1969.*

THE APOLLO MISSIONS

The United States began its journey to the moon with the start of the *Apollo* programme. The first successful, manned *Apollo* flight orbited Earth in October 1968 and sent the first live television pictures from space. In December 1968, *Apollo 8* flew to the moon and orbited it 10 times. Only seven months later, *Apollo 11* landed on the moon, and Neil Armstrong and Buzz Aldrin took their first moonwalk, becoming the first people ever to step on solid ground outside our own planet. A fifth of the world's population watched the moonwalk on live television.

▼ *The astronaut's footprint will remain on the moon forever – there is no wind to disturb the dust.*

The *Apollo* missions collected moon rock, took photographs, analyzed soil, and made many other measurements. Scientists are still making discoveries from these. In 2006, they found that moonquakes – earthquakes on the moon – are quite common. This will be taken into account when planning future moon landings.

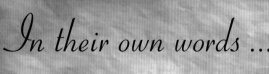

In their own words ...

❝I believe this nation should commit itself to achieve the goal, before this decade is out, of landing a man on the moon. ❞

U.S. President John F. Kennedy, 1961

APOLLO MISSIONS

1968: *Apollo 7* spends 11 days in orbit with a crew of three.

1968: *Apollo 8* takes a crew of three to the far side of the moon and orbits the moon 10 times.

1969: *Apollo 9* first tests the lander module (without landing).

1969: *Apollo 11* lands on the moon on 20 July. Neil Armstrong and Buzz (Edwin) Aldrin take the first moonwalk.

The United States has announced its ambition to build a permanent base near the moon's south pole by 2025. The first landing to prepare it would be in 2019, using an *Orion* craft.

HOW TO LAND ON THE MOON

Spacecraft like those used in the *Apollo* missions to land on the moon are made of several segments. The craft that comes back is much smaller than that which takes off, as parts are dropped once they are no longer needed.

The huge rocket needed for the launch falls away in two stages before the craft reaches orbit. The third stage puts the craft into orbit and then fires it towards the moon before it, too, falls away. The Command Service Module (CSM) and the lunar lander are carried inside the third stage. They come out and join together, then move into orbit around the moon. Finally, the lander descends to the moon's surface while the CSM stays in orbit. After the landing, part of the lander is used as a launch pad to send the other part back into orbit to dock with the CSM. The CSM fires its engine to return to Earth. As it approaches, the service module is discarded and the command module falls to Earth, protected by heat shields and parachutes for a landing in the Pacific Ocean.

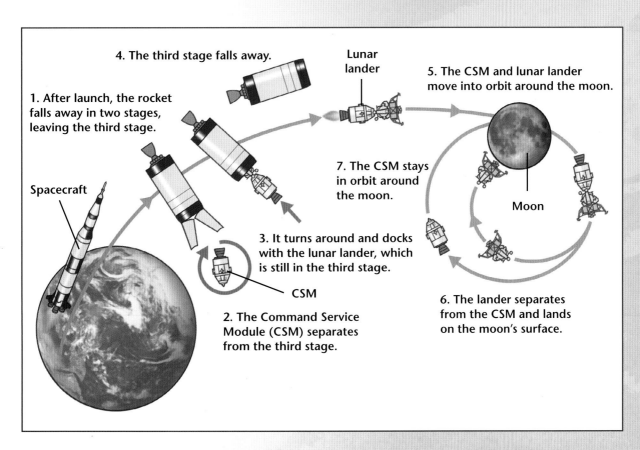

4. The third stage falls away.

Lunar lander

5. The CSM and lunar lander move into orbit around the moon.

1. After launch, the rocket falls away in two stages, leaving the third stage.

7. The CSM stays in orbit around the moon.

Spacecraft

Moon

3. It turns around and docks with the lunar lander, which is still in the third stage.

CSM

2. The Command Service Module (CSM) separates from the third stage.

6. The lander separates from the CSM and lands on the moon's surface.

WORKING IN SPACE

The *Apollo* programme ended in 1972 after six moon landings. Since then, the only human voyages into space have been to **space stations**. These are laboratories in space. Astronauts visit for several weeks or months to carry out experiments, and maintain and repair important satellites such as the Hubble Space Telescope.

The first space station was the Soviet Salyut 1, launched in 1971. After several other Salyut stations, the most famous Soviet space station, Mir, was launched in 1986. It was used extensively for experiments, observations with telescopes, and as a base from which to work on satellites. It was brought back to Earth – burning up in the atmosphere – in 2001. The only U.S. space station has been Skylab, launched in 1973 and occupied for a total of 112 days before it was abandoned. It burned up in Earth's atmosphere in 1979.

SPACE STATIONS

1971–82: Seven Salyut space stations are launched by the Soviet Union. The crew stay on board for up to a year.

1973: Skylab, the first U.S. space station, is launched. It operates for six years.

1986: Mir (Soviet Union) becomes the first space station to be assembled in space. It operates for 15 years.

1998: Construction begins on the International Space Station, due to be finished around 2010. Sixteen nations are cooperating to build it. It is already in use, even though it is not yet finished.

◄ *Astronaut Mark C. Lee takes a spacewalk against the backdrop of Earth, 240 km (150 miles) below. Astronauts have to make spacewalks like this to test new equipment or to perform maintenance work on satellites.*

WHO'S WHO

Wernher von Braun

During his childhood in Germany, Wernher von Braun (1912–77) was inspired by his interest in astronomy to investigate rockets. In the build-up to World War II, rocket research was allowed only as a way of developing weapons, and von Braun became the pioneer of German rocket technology. At the end of the war, he and his team of around 100 scientists surrendered to the U.S. Army. He launched the first U.S. satellite, *Explorer 1*, and played an important role in setting up the space programme that eventually led to the moon landings.

▼ *The Space Shuttle* Discovery *is launched in July 2006 to begin its two-day journey to the International Space Station. Seven crew members were on board.*

THE ISS

A large international team cooperated to build the International Space Station (ISS), which received its first crew in 2000. Unlike earlier space stations, which were launched from Earth, the ISS is being built in space from separately launched components. By the end of 2006, the space station had been occupied by crew for a total of 93 days.

Although space stations do not journey into space, they provide a good position from which to explore and investigate. Outside Earth's gravity and atmosphere, the conditions are ideal for some experiments and for looking out into space. Special shuttle craft are used to carry astronauts to and from space stations.

A series of space planes called Space Shuttles have also been used. First launched in 1981, these are reusable craft that look rather like a chunky aeroplane. They are launched by rocket, orbit the Earth for a period, and re-enter the atmosphere in a controlled way at the end of the mission.

PUSHING AGAINST FRONTIERS

Now that technology has taken us to the moon, the planets are the next destination for spacecraft. So far, only unmanned probes have been sent on these journeys. Probes are becoming increasingly sophisticated and are being sent on longer and more complicated journeys of discovery.

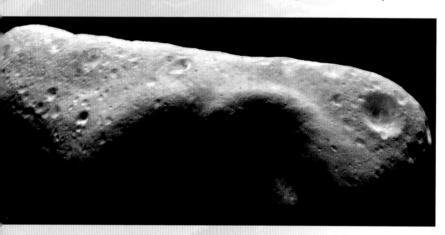

◀ *Space probes are revealing all sorts of information about space. The asteroid 433 Eros was photographed by the* NEAR-Shoemaker *probe in 2000. It revealed unusual square impact craters and many cracks. Its composition has not changed since its formation near the start of the solar system.*

CLOSE TO HOME

Mars is our most hospitable neighbour in space. Probes have shown that conditions there are more similar to those on Earth than on any other planet. This makes it the best destination for planetary exploration. The Mars Reconnaissance Orbiter took clear images of Mars in late 2006, and looked for suitable sites for future landings. The images are so detailed that features the size of a person can be seen on the surface.

NASA plans several new missions to Mars. These will examine the soil and atmosphere on Mars, drill into the surface, explore the polar ice caps, and search for evidence of past or present life. The *Phoenix* mission, due to land on Mars in 2008, will dig trenches looking for underground ice and water. The Mars Science Laboratory should be launched in 2009 and arrive on Mars in 2010.

The next significant step will be to send a craft that will collect samples from Mars and return them to Earth for investigation, or set up a robotic laboratory on Mars to investigate the possibility of life. These plans are still not fixed, but are likely to be started before 2020. There are no immediate plans to send people to Mars, but it does remain a long-term aim.

FURTHER AFIELD

Return journeys to Mars and the moon will gather valuable new information, but other missions are exploring more distant frontiers, including Mercury, Saturn, Jupiter, and some comets and asteroids.

The U.S. *Messenger* probe, launched in 2004, will go into orbit around Mercury in 2011. No probe has visited Mercury since *Mariner 10* in 1974–75. *Messenger* will investigate the side that has never been seen before, and will explore the poles. Radar from Earth shows strong echoes from the poles, which may have craters filled with ice. *Messenger* will also measure Mercury's magnetic field, to test the theory that the planet's core (which produces the magnetic field) is cooling and it is slowly collapsing.

HOLIDAYS IN SPACE

Tourists like to follow explorers to frontiers, and space is no different. Although space travel is extremely expensive, some very wealthy people have already become space tourists, paying for a flight to the International Space Station on a Russian *Soyuz* shuttle. Selling seats on space flights could become a useful source of income to support space science and exploration. Anousheh Ansari (right) became the first Muslim woman and the first Iranian to go into space. She went as a space tourist to the International Space Station for 10 days in September 2006.

INTO THE UNKNOWN

The *Voyager 1* and *2* spacecraft have now travelled further than any other object created on Earth. *Voyager 1* is already in the band at the edge of the solar system called the **heliosheath**, where the sun has little influence. The solar wind in the heliosheath is slower, thicker, and hotter than it is inside the solar system. If a person were on *Voyager 1*, the sun would look only one ten-thousandth as bright as it does from Earth.

Voyager measures the speed and magnetic fields of the solar wind, and the waves and particles that make it up. It sends radio broadcasts of the sound of the solar wind back to Earth (recordings of solar wind are available online, see page 44). It will take 10 years for *Voyager 1* to pass through the heliosheath. It should finally leave the solar system around 2016. NASA hopes to keep contact with the craft until 2020.

CURRENT AND FUTURE MISSIONS

2007: *New Horizons* will return photographs of Jupiter on its way to Pluto and the Kuiper Belt.

2007: Launch of *Dawn*, set to orbit two of the largest asteroids, Vesta (in 2011) and Ceres (in 2014). This is the first probe to use ion propulsion.

2010: Proposed launch of *Juno* to orbit Jupiter, looking for evidence of an ice-rock core, to work out how much water and ammonia are present, and to study winds.

2011: *Messenger* will enter orbit around Mercury.

2014: The ESA probe *Rosetta* will land on Comet 67P/ Churyumov-Gerasimenko.

▲ *Light from the Pleiades, a cluster of stars 400 light years from Earth, is captured by a telescope. From the bands of light, scientists can work out the chemical composition of the stars.*

MESSAGES FROM SPACE

Space exploration is not only about venturing from Earth to cross new frontiers. Scientists also gather information coming from deep space. This includes radio waves, background radiation, and microwaves, as well as the light picked up by optical telescopes. We can learn a lot about distant stars and galaxies and about the history of the universe from these sources.

READING STARS

Scientists work out what stars are made of by looking at **spectra** – patterns that show the brightness of the object at many different wavelengths. Radio telescopes have vast reflective dishes to collect radio signals from space. **X-ray** telescopes on satellites orbiting Earth collect X-rays sent out by galaxy clusters and by compact stars such as **neutron stars** and **black holes**. The power of the X-rays from these stars is thousands of times stronger than the light. Some of the information scientists are gathering now left its source near the beginning of the universe. It tells us as much about distant times as about distant places.

▲ *This galaxy cluster is Stephan's Quintet. The image was taken using a special camera from the Calar Alto Observatory in Spain.*

▼ *The vast receiving dishes of this radio telescope system pick up signals from deep space. The dish focuses the radio waves on to a reflector (suspended over the middle of the dish), which directs them to a receiver.*

LIFE ON OTHER WORLDS

For centuries people have dreamed of – and feared – life on other planets. Scientists are looking for evidence of life in the solar system, but expect to find microbes rather than strange-looking monsters. If there is anything larger, it is probably far away.

LIFE ON MARS?

All forms of life we know of depend on water in one way or another. If there is water on a moon or planet, there might also be life there.

In science fiction and films, aliens have often come from Mars. There is water on Mars – there are features created by flowing water, such as dried riverbeds, and some of these have appeared in the last seven years. There is underground ice, and may be vast oceans locked beneath the surface of Mars. Meteorites from Mars 3.6 billion years old might contain fossilized micro-organisms. A newly discovered set of underground caves seems to have both water and a more stable temperature than the surface. These could possibly host life. Future missions to the planet will carry out soil experiments designed to look for evidence of any life forms.

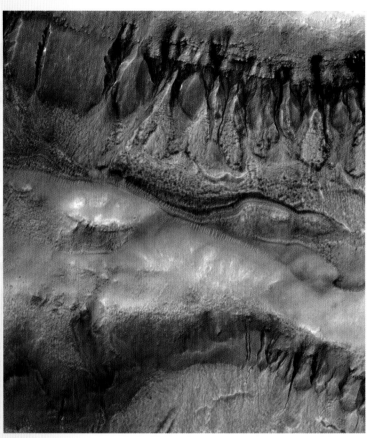

▲ Landforms like this gully on Mars suggest that there is water on the planet. The channels on the walls of the gully have been made by seeping liquid.

SETI AND THE SEARCH FOR INTELLIGENT LIFE

Radio telescopes collect a huge amount of data from distant galaxies. The Search for Extra-Terrestrial Intelligence, or SETI, scans all the radio signals received for patterns that might suggest they were sent by intelligent beings. Anyone can download the SETI@Home computer program. When the computer is turned on but not being used, the program searches for patterns in a section of the radio data gathered by telescopes. If a pattern is found, the result is sent back to SETI over the Internet.

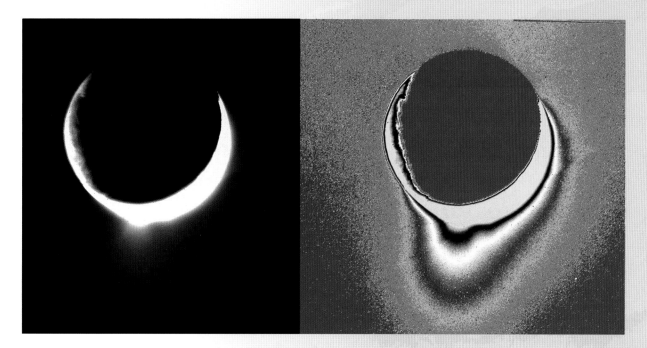

▲ *Ice jets on Saturn's moon Enceladus send particles streaming into space above its south pole. This image was taken by the* Cassini *spacecraft. The left-hand side shows the original image; the right-hand side has been colour-enhanced to show the ice jets more clearly.*

MICROBES IN SPACE

Microbes can survive in very hostile conditions – they have survived trips to the moon and the space station. On Earth, life has been found in such extreme environments as deep under the ocean, inside volcanic vents, beneath the polar ice, and in deep mine shafts. Perhaps some of the planets that were once thought too hostile to support life may in fact be inhabited.

LIFE ON OTHER MOONS?

Could there be life on moons instead of planets? Scientists have now investigated Earth's moon sufficiently thoroughly to be fairly sure there is no life there. But in 2006, the probe *Cassini* took pictures of an ice volcano on a moon of Saturn – Enceladus – which appears to erupt water. If there is liquid water on Enceladus, there is a chance of life there.

Some people believe that life on Earth originated in space, and that microbes carried on meteorites "seeded" the planet with primitive life forms. Most scientists dismiss the idea, but some claim to have found microbes at the very top of Earth's atmosphere, which they believe could have come from space.

OTHER WORLDS

No one knows how many stars there are in the universe. Some scientists believe there may be between 200 and 400 billion stars just in the Milky Way, and perhaps 10 billion trillion (10 followed by 22 zeroes) in the entire universe. Any of these stars could have a number of planets, and some of those planets could support life. It seems unlikely that we occupy the only inhabited planet in the universe.

COMMUNICATING WITH SPACE

If there are other life forms in space, could we contact them? Communication is a two-way process. While we are looking for radio signals that may come from other life forms, beings on distant planets may be picking up our radio signals.

In 1974, the Arecibo telescope on Puerto Rico sent out a coded message towards the M13 star cluster. Intelligent beings should be able to decode it into pictures showing a human figure, the telescope itself, the solar system, and the shape of the **DNA** molecule. M13 contains 300,000 stars, any of which might have inhabited planets. It is 21,000 light years away, though, so the earliest we could expect a reply is in 42,000 years' time.

MESSAGE IN A BOTTLE

The *Voyager* spacecraft carry gold-plated disks containing images and sounds from Earth. They include music, sounds of animals and weather, and spoken greetings in 55 languages, including one last spoken 6,000 years ago in Sumeria. The instructions for playing the disk are shown in symbols.

MOVING OUT

Wanting to colonize new areas has always been a reason for pioneers to explore frontiers. One reason for space exploration is to search for other habitable worlds. We might want to live on other planets for several reasons, just as people move to different countries on Earth for many reasons. One would be the excitement and adventure of living elsewhere in space. Early colonies may spring up on planets or moons where we can gather resources such as metals or fuels, or grow food – just as frontiersmen on Earth have searched for precious resources and farmed new lands.

◄ *The* Voyager *craft have on board gold-plated disks, inscribed with diagrams that explain the history of Earth. If the craft are ever found by other beings on their journey into deep space, it is hoped they will be able to understand these inscriptions and learn about life on Earth.*

MAKING A NEW HOME

We are a long way from having a new planet to inhabit, but people have begun investigating planetary engineering, or **terraforming**. This is the modelling and engineering of a new world to suit our needs. It would mean providing water, a surface we can live on, an atmosphere we can breathe, food and drink, and a temperature that could support animal and plant life.

LOOKING FOR NEW WORLDS

NASA's *Kepler* mission, due to launch in 2008, will use a telescope anchored in space to scan the galaxy for planets about the same size as Earth that could support life. Over four years, it will look at an area of sky about the size of a human hand held at arm's length, monitoring 100,000 stars. It will watch for the dimming of a star as a planet crosses in front of it. From repeated readings for each star, it will work out the size of the planet, its orbit, and its distance from the star.

▼ *An artist's impression of a station on Mars, where people might live at some time in the future. The Mars sky can have an orange-red tint when storms have thrown dust into the atmosphere.*

WHOSE UNIVERSE IS IT?

Crossing frontiers has always raised moral questions. What rights do we have in new territories? Early human pioneers often abused and exploited both human and animal inhabitants of the places they explored. Are we in danger of doing the same in space? If there are other living beings in the universe, what rights do we have beyond our own planet? What harm might we do by visiting other worlds and sending objects into space? Should we be going into space at all?

▼ Parts of the lunar module Antares, from the Apollo 14 moon landing, remain on the surface of the moon. Debris from all moon landings can be found in different places on the lunar surface.

WHY ARE WE GOING?

Humans have always had the urge to explore new frontiers, to discover new knowledge, and inhabit new areas. Space exploration is part of our greater quest for understanding and knowledge about ourselves, our own world, and its place in the universe. Looking at other planets in the solar system may reveal how life evolved on Earth and how our planet works. Looking deep into space may tell us about the origins of the universe itself.

There are, however, less honourable reasons for venturing into space. Although it resulted in valuable technological advances and significant milestones in our understanding of space, the space race in the 1960s between the United States and the Soviet Union was motivated by national pride and international hostility. Modern exploration may be spurred on by the desire for commercial gain – to make money out of resources that could be taken from other planets – or to place weapons in space.

SHOULD WE EXPLORE SPACE?

Some people argue that the huge cost of space travel is not worth the small gain we have seen so far. Much good could be done on Earth, fighting disease, starvation, poverty, injustice, and climate change with the money that is spent on space exploration. There are still unexplored areas on Earth that are easier, safer, and cheaper to investigate. Perhaps we should concentrate on these first.

On the other hand, scientists promoting the space programmes say that in the future we will reap great benefits from the investment in space exploration, and that it will greatly increase our understanding of our own planet.

SPACE JUNK

As spacecraft travel around the solar system, they leave bits of craft and equipment on other planets and in orbit around Earth, other planets, and the sun. This space junk will not rust or rot away. It is causing increasing problems for satellites and astronauts.

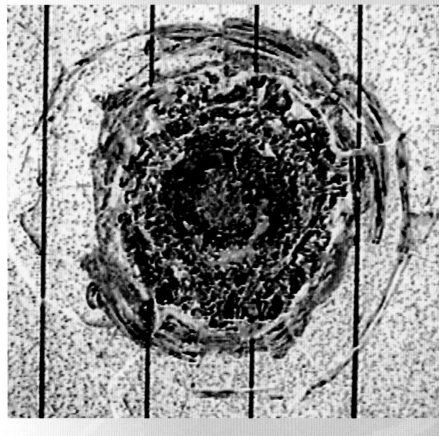

▼ *Space junk can damage satellites. This crater in a solar panel of the Hubble Space Telescope was probably caused by a collision with debris from a previous spacecraft.*

If humans disappeared from Earth tomorrow, destroyed by war, disease, or a natural disaster, all trace that we had ever been here would be gone after about 100,000 years – yet our junk on the moon would remain. Already, one piece of space junk in orbit over Earth has caused an accident when a satellite crashed into it. Is it right to leave our debris on other planets and moons, where it might one day affect developing life, or be found by other, alien, space travellers?

As Earth struggles to cope with its own rubbish, and in particular its radioactive waste, some people have suggested firing toxic waste into the sun. There, it would be destroyed and can no longer harm us. It should be broken down without trace, the atoms stripped apart and turned into the hydrogen ions that are produced by the sun. Is it right to do this, or should we be making more effort to find ways of dealing with our waste here on Earth – or stop producing it altogether?

UNKNOWN RISKS

Wherever we travel, we take microbes from Earth. They have been found on the moon from previous landings and survive on the outside of space stations. Leaving microbes from Earth on other planets and moons we visit could interfere with life that is starting there. By polluting habitats in this way, we may do untold damage without knowing it.

Our searches for life are for life forms we recognize, but it is possible that life forms we do not recognize are present, and could be affected by our visits, by what we leave behind – and even by what we take away.

SPACE FOR EVERYONE

Space exploration has been carried out only by wealthy nations. Russia (and formerly the Soviet Union), the United States, Europe, and Japan have played a part. India and China are smaller players so far, although China's space expertise is growing quickly. There are many people in the world who are not represented at all. Who will "own" the areas discovered? Can one nation lay claim to parts of another planet and stop others exploring or exploiting it? Already some businesses are "selling" land on the moon and Mars, even though they have no legal title to it.

SEEK AND DESTROY

Human space exploration should be peaceful – yet already scientists have sent probes to crash deliberately into the surface of planets, moons, comets, and asteroids. The purpose of these experiments is to measure the shockwaves produced and reveal information about the composition of the body. But is it right to damage other objects in space intentionally, even if we believe them to be uninhabited?

▼ Endeavor, *the last of the five U.S. Space Shuttles, landing on its return to Earth. Launched in 1992, it is a reusable spacecraft used to deliver astronauts and components to the International Space Station. It may be that in time everyone will be able to fly to the moon on a future version of the Space Shuttle, the way we might take a flight to another country.*

ARMCHAIR ASTRONAUTS

New stars and comets have often been found by amateurs with home-based telescopes. Space, though it remains the final frontier, is opening up to more and more would-be explorers of all ages. Since the mid-1990s video feeds from space probes have been available on the Internet, so that everyone can follow the progress of these missions and share the excitement of discovery through images from the furthest reaches of the solar system. Modern space missions give us all the chance to be explorers, seeing the surface of distant planets instantly, as it is revealed for the first time. Even more, programs such as SETI@Home and Stardust give anyone with a computer the chance to be involved personally, helping to sift through the masses of space data looking for the tiny clues that will lead us on the next steps in our joint journey to the stars.

▲ *Equipment such as this rover was left scattered around the moon landing sites by the* Apollo *missions. It will not deteriorate as it would on Earth.*

FACTS AND STATISTICS

THE SUN, MOON, AND PLANETS

THE SUN
Average temperature (core): 15,000,000°C (27,000,000°F)
Average temperature (surface): 5,800°C (10,470°F)
Diameter: 1,500,000,000 km (932,000,000 miles)
Mass: 333,000 x Earth
Rotation period: 25–34 Earth days

MERCURY
Average temperature: 167°C (333°F)
Diameter: 4,879 km (3,032 miles)
Distance from sun: 0.387 AU
Mass: 0.05 x Earth
Year: 88 Earth days
Day: 58.8 Earth days

VENUS
Average temperature: 464°C (867°F)
Diameter:12,104 km (7,521 miles)
Distance from sun: 0.723 AU
Mass: 0.82 x Earth
Year: 224.7 Earth days
Day: 243 Earth days

EARTH
Average temperature: 15°C (59°F)
Diameter: 12,756 km (7,926 miles)
Distance from sun: 1 AU
Year: 365.25 Earth days
Day: 24 hours

MOON
Average temperature: –20°C (–4°F)
Diameter: 3,475 km (2,159 miles)
Mass: 0.012 x Earth
Orbital period: 27.3 Earth days

MARS
Average temperature: –63°C (–81°F)
Diameter: 6,794 km (4,222 miles)
Distance from sun: 1.524 AU
Mass: 0.11 x Earth
Year: 687 Earth days
Day: 1.03 Earth days

JUPITER
Average temperature: –110°C (–166°F)
Diameter: 142,984 km (88,846 miles)
Distance from sun: 5.203 AU
Mass: 318 x Earth
Year: 11.88 Earth years
Day: 0.41 Earth days

SATURN
Average temperature: –140°C (–220°F)
Diameter: 120,536 km (74,898 miles)
Distance from sun: 9.529 AU
Mass: 95 x Earth
Year: 29.46 Earth years
Day: 0.44 Earth days

URANUS
Average temperature: –195°C (–319°F)
Diameter: 51,118 km (31,763 miles)
Distance from sun: 19.19 AU
Mass: 14.5 x Earth
Year: 84 Earth years
Day: 0.72 Earth days

NEPTUNE
Average temperature: –200°C (–328°F)
Diameter: 49,528 km (30,775 miles)
Distance from sun: 30.06 AU
Mass: 17.1 x Earth
Year: 164.9 Earth years
Day: 0.67 Earth days

SPACE EXPLORATION

UNMANNED EXPLORATION

First satellite to go into orbit: *Sputnik 1*, Soviet Union, 4 October 1957

First object to escape Earth orbit: *Luna 1*, Soviet Union, 2 January 1959 (moon flyby)

First unmanned moon landing: *Luna 2*, Soviet Union, 14 September 1959 (deliberate impact with the moon)

PEOPLE IN SPACE

First human in space: Yuri Gagarin in *Vostok 1*, Soviet Union, 12 April 1961; remained in space 1 hour 48 minutes

First woman in space: Valentina Tereshkova in *Vostok 6*, Soviet Union, 16 June 1963

First fatal space accident: Vladimir Komarov, Soviet Union, killed when *Soyuz 1* crashed returning to Earth, 24 April 1967

First humans on the moon: Neil Armstrong and Edwin (Buzz) Aldrin in *Apollo 11*, United States, 20 July 1969

First permanently manned space station: Mir, Soviet Union, in orbit 1986–2001

First space tourist: Dennis Tito, United States, visits the International Space Station, 28 April 2001

EXPLORING THE PLANETS

First probe to hit another planet: *Venera 3* impacted with Venus, 1 March 1966 (launched 16 November 1965)

First data received from the surface of another planet: *Venera 7*, Soviet Union, transmitted data from Venus, 15 December 1970 (launched 17 August 1970)

First probe to land on Mars: *Mars 2*, Soviet Union, 27 November 1971

First complete mapping of another planet: *Magellan*, United States, mapped 98 percent of the surface of Venus, 1990–92

ENCOUNTERING ASTEROIDS

First asteroid flyby: *Galileo*, United States, 1991, photographed 951 Gaspra, first close-up photographs of an asteroid

First spacecraft to land on an asteroid: *NEAR-Shoemaker*, United States, 2001, landed on 433 Eros

First probe to take samples from an asteroid: *Hayabusa*, Japan, November 2005 (it is not known for certain whether any sample has been successfully retrieved – the probe is expected to return to Earth in 2010)

FINAL FRONTIERS

First spacecraft to leave the solar system: *Voyager 1*, United States, launched 5 September 1977, began crossing the edge of the solar system 2006

Most distant man-made object: *Voyager 1*, United States

FURTHER RESOURCES

BOOKS

A Visual Encyclopedia of Space, Robin Kerrod, Dorling Kindersley, 2006

Can We Travel to the Stars?, Rosalind Mist and Andrew Solway, Heinemann Library, 2006

e.explore: Space Travel, Ian Graham, Dorling Kindersley, 2006

Exploring Space, Gregory L. Vogt, Raintree, 2003

Home on the Moon: Living on a Space Frontier, Marianne Dyson, National Geographic Books, 2003

The Moon Landing, Nigel Kelly, Heinemann Library, 2006

Voyages Through Time: Escape from the Earth, Peter Ackroyd, Dorling Kindersley, 2004

WEBSITES

www.nasa.gov/vision/space/features/
NASA's page about manned space travel

www.nasa.gov/vision/universe/features/
NASA's page about space outside the solar system

www.bbc.co.uk/science/space/
Lots of information about space and space travel, including interactive games to test your knowledge

http://setiathome.ssl.berkeley.edu/
Download the SETI@home software so that your computer can take part in the search for extra-terrestrial life

http://stardustathome.ssl.berkeley.edu/
Download the Stardust@home software to help look for particles of interstellar dust in the Stardust sample

http://voyager.jpl.nasa.gov/050523-voyager.qtl
Listen to the solar wind, relayed from *Voyager 1*

GLOSSARY

analyse look at something in detail to understand its features

armillary sphere instrument made up of rings to form a sphere, used to work out the orbits of the planets

asteroid large lump of rock or iron orbiting the sun

Asteroid Belt area of our solar system between Mars and Jupiter, where lots of asteroids orbit

astronaut person who voyages into space (American/Western term)

Astronomical Unit (AU) unit used to measure distances in space. One AU is the distance from Earth to the sun.

axis imaginary line through the middle of a body, around which it spins

black hole star that has collapsed into itself, becoming small but very dense. Its gravity is so strong that not even light can escape from it, making it appear black.

comet chunk of rock, dust, and ice orbiting the sun, which has a long, streaming tail of gas and dust that always points towards the sun

constellation area of the sky as divided by the International Astronomical Union. There are 88 constellations.

cosmonaut person who voyages into space (Soviet/Russian term)

DNA (deoxyribonucleic acid) chemical that makes up the genetic material of all known living things on Earth

electromagnetic radiation waves of energy with electric and magnetic components. Depending on the waves' frequency (from the lowest), they may form radio waves, microwaves, infrared, visible light, ultra-violet, or X-rays.

European Space Agency (ESA) European space research and exploration organization, founded in 1975

flyby mission that flies past a planet or moon

galaxy huge collection of stars

gas giant large planet made mostly of chemicals that exist as a gas at the temperatures and pressures on Earth

gravitational field area around a body such as a planet where its gravity influences other bodies

gravity force acting between any two masses or bodies. It is gravity that holds planets in their orbits.

heliosheath zone on the very outer reaches of the solar system

heliospheric relating to the heliosphere – the area around the sun where the influence of the solar wind extends

imager equipment for making images of features of planets, working from different types of electromagnetic radiation including light, radio waves, X-rays, and infrared radiation

immune system body's method of fighting infection and disease

infrared form of **electromagnetic radiation**

interstellar between stars

ion atom or group of atoms that has an electrical charge

ion propulsion method of powering a spacecraft using a stream of high-energy ions

Kuiper Belt area on the outer limits of the solar system, beyond Neptune's orbit, made up of icy bodies

lander module that lands on a planet to carry out exploration

light pollution dim illumination of the night sky by artificial light, such as street lamps, making it difficult to see objects in space

light year distance travelled by light in one year. Light travels at nearly 300,000 km (186,400 miles) per second, so one light year is approximately 9.5 trillion km (5.9 trillion miles).

mass measure of how much matter an object contains

meteor chunk of rock glowing in the atmosphere as it falls to Earth

meteorite chunk of rock from space that has fallen to Earth

meteoroid small chunk of rock in space

microbe tiny organisms, such as bacteria

moon large body of rock or ice that orbits a planet

neutron star star that has become greatly compressed and is only about 10–20 km (6–12 miles) across. They eventually become black holes.

Oort Cloud spherical cloud of comets, thought to extend half way to the nearest neighbouring star, Proxima Centauri

optical working with light

orbit movement of a star or planet, held in a circular or elliptical path by gravity

photon packet of light energy, sharing some of the properties of a particle and some of a wave

pioneer someone who explores unknown places

planet large body of rock or gas that orbits a star (including the sun) and is large enough to have sufficient gravity to have swept in and absorbed other smaller bodies near it

planetoid (dwarf planet) body orbiting a star, which is large enough to have sufficient gravity to be nearly round, but not sufficient to have swept in all smaller bodies near it

probe unmanned spacecraft

radar use of radio waves to discover the shape or presence of objects. Radio waves are bounced off the surface, and the reflection is measured by a radio receiver to show a surface or detect objects.

radiation energy emitted as waves or particles

radioactive property of emitting radiation

radio wave form of electromagnetic radiation

satellite body that orbits a planet. Moons are natural satellites; artificial satellites include tools built to help with communications, mapping, national security, and to hold space stations and telescopes.

scarp long, steep slope

solar system system of the sun, planets, moons, and other bodies orbiting the sun

solar wind thinly distributed particles that come from the sun and are sent out into space

sound wave pressure waves that pass through the air or other material, which to the human ear produce sounds

space race competition between the United States and the Soviet Union to conquer space in the 1950s, 1960s, and 1970s

space station spacecraft in orbit around Earth that astronauts visit to carry out experiments and observations

spacewalk trip into space from a spacecraft made by an astronaut in a spacesuit, but not using a vehicle. The astronaut may be tethered to the spacecraft.

spectra the range of colours emitted by an object

sphere three-dimensional circle – all its edges are the same distance from the central point

terraforming also known as planetary engineering. A theory about altering the atmosphere of a planet or moon to make it habitable for humans.

terrestrial relating to, or like, Earth

turbulence rapid variations in pressure and speed in the atmosphere that can cause storms

ultraviolet form of electromagnetic radiation

wavelength distance between the peaks of two successive waves. Different wavelengths result in different colours of light.

X-ray form of electromagnetic radiation

INDEX